Urchin to Follow

Urchin to Follow

Dorine Jennette

The National Poetry Review Press

The National Poetry Review Press
(an imprint of DHP)
Post Office Box 2080, Aptos, California 95001-2080

author photo by Rachel Whalley

Printed in the United States of America
Published in 2010 by The National Poetry Review Press

978-0-9821155-7-2
Library of Congress Control Number: 2010923487

Cover art:
Sea Urchin
Oil on masonite, 27"x 24"
Patricia Figueroa
http://www.patriciafigueroa.com/

for Dorje, who wasn't surprised

CONTENTS

1

What makes the engine go?
Desire, desire, desire.

—Stanley Kunitz

Ode to Doubt

Muscle of boa, you turn
smooth as cognac stilled
fifty years in the throat.
You muffle hard outlines
under your skirts,
offer a grey handkerchief
to each certainty.
Behind the civility of veils—
what manners! You understand
how vulgar clarity can be.
At your discretion,
the lampshade's tassels.
Yours, the axe swung wide.
You own the dog afloat
on the ocean, the blurred print
on the dog's sodden collar.
You shake the hand
that finds a cold canary,
burning lung that must inhale.
Smudge-mouthed last child
left in the parking lot.
Dead horse, middle fork,
gloved hands in hair.

Marriage Song in the Desert

Therefore the cicada groans at evening,
flame in the sky luring flame
from the earth's orange blossoms,
trumpet vine and oleander leaning on a fence,
Come and find me perched on the dark, dense
branch of a dwarf peach tree. For it's really
a sexual pleasure, isn't it, to hold
a ripening peach, still on the branch, in one's hand?
The warm water-weight of it, the downy skin
like an earlobe between the lips.
Did I just catch you staring at my hips?
Each brush of your hand at the base of my throat
begs and offers surrender at a stroke,
for the desert is full of doors:
blue-painted wood buoyed by adobe's warm hands;
pink bricks relaxing ridge into notch;
the beams of the old miner's cabin
still strong, still folded into stone.
Red steel plates rise in arroyos
to release irrigation's miracle,
and we are called to walk through every gate.
Your hand at the blush of my throat
calls my breath buoyant, carries me to you
across this bridge we leap from,
falling through a panoply of doors.

For how could you have found me, lover,
if the owl's ghost-zooming had not circled the pines,
if the cottonwood did not lead us to water?
Dragonfly and cricket are lucky, you say,
in their craving for flight's long fall, the yield
of each cascade to land. Lucky, the dragonfly
and cricket, our guides to mesquite and acacia,
to the barrel cactus full of gravid fire.
We are growing sharp; we are holding on to water;
we are our own peach tree,
our own stone gate and wooden door.

To the Rescue Crew

Open me up
with the jaws of life,
you'll find I'm full
of fish: the deep-
sea kind, whose
dewlaps dredge a trench.
Minding their veils
of milk silt and slime,
my bulge-eyed denizens
sound their scales.
It's the pressure
does it, and the dark.

Ode to the Tune of Frank O'Hara

Oh phone! You are a sleek silver super-
huge bullet in the palm! Allowing me
to believe I am Clint Eastwood
when I am only calling the dentist!
But perhaps I should not squint into
the wind this way (certainly such chomping
on cigars is bad for me). It will not do
to confuse my office with a desert!
Maybe some dry weed will tumble me
to Vegas, where every long leg swings
from a lit-up brick. How short-
lived is beauty in the absence
of preservative liquids! I order seabreeze
after seabreeze from a Cleopatra
I'm not sure how to tip—how can I multiply
in the presence of false eyelashes?—and each tide
arrives in a glass I don't know. Perfectly crimped
trouser cuffs everywhere! This current
of smooth men in smooth suits that breaks
around the polyester-shadowed slot machines
leaves sand in my shoes and that's why
I'm kicking off my knickers
to shimmy up the nearest palm tree
and from the top I'll dial until someone understands.

Road Trip

Naturally, we won't get what we want.
While we drive stinking down the mountain
to shuck the pleasures of snow-covered yucca
and cottonwood for imminent enchiladas,
the radio reveals that this year's migrating monarchs
died in a freak storm in Mexico, their million
yellow and black wings blurred to a single flag.
The old truck's heater whines; the father at the wheel
confides he hopes his wife forgets the worst
of childbirth's ring of fire—
Sunday night in a desert town: everything is closed
to us, and to imago Io moths, who have no mouths,
who mate and starve, whose children do the same,
while mechanics in Cuba, lacking parts, keep 1950s
American cars running strong on rubberbands
and spit, what a machinist can make fit.
Gravity will have us all eventually,
so each of the desert's great balancing stones
perches on its tiny base. As tumbleweeds skate
over rabbits and beetles, we revive an old debate,
and fogging the windows with our cant,
a Jack Mormon, an atheist, and a militant agnostic
are mindful that every desire is a winding sheet.
We want better breath, the last cracker, to bloom
with the barrel cactus by the road's shoulder,

or, emerged from the canyon's shelter,
exposed to the stars and the radio's reminders
of those to whom we return, we long
to lick the neck of the person nearest us.

Advice

Is it
the sight—ripe
strawberry—or
biting

that gives
pleasure? Burst
juice or each hard
green seed?

I don't
need to know
this — she sighs for
a married

friend who
touched her hair,
once, perfectly—
how he

would touch
everything
else, which of course
he won't.

18

Patience?
Potential
is its own event.
Perverse,

some autumn
leaves won't fall,
but hang on 'til
spring, or

evap-
orate one
gold fleck at a
time. Meanwhile,

she leans
on a birch
trunk; brittle pen-
dulum

sways, shakes
above her
cupped, her gentle
hand. Step

away
from the tree.

Tracking the Woodcutter

Woodsmoke. Dawn in Montana. Above the boot-
print's crust, the bark—here, where the blade scored
out—an accusation. White-gold splinters of hair.

By the lake, he flung my hatchet into the woods. My
axe was too small, too—end over end, it hummed
toward pine and buried itself in sap. Trees, he shat-
tered with a maul and sledge until the blade-edge
razed the summer air. There was sweetness when
he wielded weapons: always the sweat at the small
of his back, beading on fine fuzz, the corrugated
honey of his spine. Always six grooves of sinew—his
whittled waist—between myself and his spleen.

Here is his campfire dying in snow, the overturned
sled smashed for fuel.

Anniversary Sale Specials

Such as the half moon like a baby's head, crown-
ing. Sometime like a three-legged stool. Wicker and
wrought-iron chairs get ready to mumble about
the garden party's doilies, mackerel tatting and
lye. Swallows flutter by sheets on the line as cheap
quiche flies off the shelves. A hall of frozen doors
stores mountain storms in the radio, to keep.

Always buy a button-closure tent. If you want
origami with sound, tack a bent ear to the ground,
green concrete in a butterfly's shade. Via catalog,
a flock of them swilling, drunk on a pile of dung:
you can't buy grace by degrees. You lose a face by
degrees, everything sunk but the eyes and teeth,
gone down. Take a half pound, sliced thin. On sale,
good thing.

Gringos Lost in the Sonoran Desert

Left hand vaguely toward his shoulder,
she asks him what's left to discuss, points out
a vaquero's cow-pony, sturdy and smart,
as they bounce down a dirt washboard
in their aging, no-clearance van.
Tin-roofed shacks present their doors
of blacksmithed cacti, chiseled wood.
She is tired of picturesque failures,
of the grit that sits in her throat,
yet she observes their rearview
plume of sand above the axles' chatter.
Cicadas chant in the riot-high grass,
then a gap in the green and he guns it
toward the small river
splashing through the road—
the local swimming hole,
rigged with rope swings for swift children.
Their dust follows them as they drop and stall;
old rope creaks over reeds.
Knee deep and confused,
they practice fractured apologies:
"Lo siento." "Lo siento por todo."
They rest themselves in the shallows.

Strategy

Maybe I'll tie myself to the mast, wax rhapsodic as
snippets of *Like, for sure* assail the library lounge.
Each sharpens, proliferates a flock of points,
fletches syringes, I am needled, isn't that a goad?
As *insiduous* might mean suspicious trees, I advertise
rhubarb pies to a coastline of anorexics, or I peddle
lipstick to starfish under the dock, serenading their
hollow tube feet.

Home Economics

Lately, less ringing in the tea tin:
fewer phones, for fur prefers quiet,

cold, cups without thumbs.
Clappers from bells set to fry,

I ignore the door's conjectures,
reply only please help yourself

to a wreath of pink purslane—
fourth from the right on the stoop.

In this room, let there be facts
no fat can pacify.

I dream in antlers and chest wounds.
Yes, yes, I'm sixteen again.

Goose on the mailbox, onion under stool,
no chowder can come of this,

and so many irons in the fire!
A good landing is one you walk away from.

Homecoming Weekend

The backyard hammock cradles mist
and falling leaves that settle into the swaying mesh.
Down the street, the frat boys are building a float,
all shout and hustle, and one last wasp
dies on the lawn, invites me

to step down barefoot. I'll walk
to the vending machine on the corner, where,
for your quarters, you might be offered one or two
of anything—guaranteed to be cold and fizzy,
but rarely what you thought you'd get. Maybe God

is not so much a clock winder
as a vending machine, dispensing bounty
without regard for brand, deaf to requests.
It hums and gurgles to itself
in the darkness, choosing for us.

What the Evening Requires

It's a rare soul who loves lawnmowers, so
someone has braided the long grass
downslope to the street, complete
with bright bows; oh, gather the ends
like the tails of showhorses and schoolgirls!
For perhaps it's this beacon
leading the out-of-place pelicans
too far north along a fall-crisping coast:
huge, they maintain formation
a foot above the shore's
breakers. Dark surf flings up its capers of foam,
effervescent as the legs of the volleyball player
who vaults skyward for each overhand smash,
whose bursts are borrowed
from the drifted log's bleached bones
on which my brother, the mad king,
props his foot to take pictures of holes in the sand
and of wind-ripped, unbraided beach grass,
a cold cigarette between his lips
for the way it plaits the wind.

Possible Song

Song of the wine between bottle and glass,
song of the gate, unlatched,
the winding stair. Song of the mist
over any mountain pass, song of the opening bars.

The first skipped beat. Song of the spider's
turn around the copper clock tower, greening.
The hinge's screed, the purpling urchin and fig.
The oil leak steams.

Song of swallows flung from a pine,
song of the talon's balm.
Song of the bent leg's urgent repose,
song on one wing, flexed.

Song of the welder's rising mask.
The warm dough lofts
and the loom hums to the lathe.
Chipped song dropped from a chiseled lip,

wet song leaning on a breast.
Song of the bouquet slung over the bull's horns,
song of the bee's plumping thighs.
Song of sugar that ends in sand.

Song of the bow wave, the lookout's cry,
song of the wax toward words.

Margins

In winter one madrona leans
to drop Orion's body from its snag,
where "sword" and "sea cliff"
share the root

he is sliding over,
the *ecg* or "edge,"
blade spilled
from his loosening

grasp—from *grāp*,
pronounced "grape."
Pebbles flicked
in the wind

sing on a wineglass's lip,
sting the hands
in his hair, a pelt
as thick as a mink's.

Stance

If, therefore, hesitation is danger — doubt
pulsed through each limb's decision —

then I am shaken at the twig's tip
where wind wrings the tree's

high branches to start the sap.
I live at the lip

where the ripe pecan pants
at the opening pod's edge —

a claw, a quadranted womb,
a loosening compass blown

beyond the magnet's knowledge,
spun past any certainty.

The ground so far.

Narrative

The back porch is no place to look for relief.
I never trust the new spring sun, nor bees,
those local drunks, buzzes guttering like the engine

of a rusty fishing boat full throttle
for a beer at The Rotten Mullet,
"Hammer Dan" at the tiller cursing

for lack of a decent bilge pump—
the bees, to which I am so allergic,
remind me periodically

that only trouble is interesting, which may be why
bees give directions by dance. It's breezy here
despite the bees' reminder that I carry this big needle

for a reason, last seen in Cochise Stronghold, AZ.
The name's a clue that there's been trouble there.
Up at four, we'd stumble into yuccas on our way

to our packs, and briefly curse, inhaling bagels
as we hiked to climb the crags,
then early call it quits and spend the late day

drinking beer and eating spicy chips, playing cards

and listening to somebody not bad on the guitar.
In this, we resembled young narratives,

whose long legs sprawl backward and forward,
teenagers who colonize a couch,
leaving big kicked-off shoes to linger in the mind.

Tied in at the third belay, I reached to scratch my back
and caught a stinger in my thumb
for an allergic person's etymological thrill:

anaphylaxis binds the roots of *up, back, again,* and *guard*—
by which we learn the body is a bureaucrat commanding
a war, who orders a charge and retreat at once,

so that its parts attack each other in passing.
Since the needle's a spring-loaded kit,
one stab in the thigh does the job,

and, suffocation averted, we had
our biggest trouble with a twin-spotted rattlesnake
coiled under the ends of our ropes.

Whereas, this afternoon from my backyard
where my fat cat tramples the pansies,
I've risked only a quick stick

and a sweaty race to the hospital,
plus injections with soporific drugs

that would have caused me to take a nap

during which I might have dreamt of other things,
such as touring Rome as a roadie
and leaping into the driver's seat of a no-brakes

band bus down a cobbled hill gaining on three children
(two girls and a boy) on bicycles. *Avanti!*
As you see, I might have lost this train of thought.

There are worse ways to spend an afternoon
than perched on the porch daydreaming narrative poems.
So many fights I could have started

with the people I love, given these few hours.
Yes, I'm sure there's some lame wreckage
I could have made that would even now

be limping along on its assorted twigs,
shambling, with the shattered ends
of its hands in its mouth, down the street.

2

Only a handful of girls grows to awareness
of the dark silence exactly at the center of the wedding —
the missing piece of the lace puzzle only separation will fit.

—Donna Stonecipher

You

God, I could put out
your eyes I could
put out. I could wring
my hands, my snakes.

There it is, damn its stench:
the error house.
Yes, you embarrass me,
you easy liquor.

I'm done dredging gutters
for honeysuckle,
for the dumb fuzz from your thighs—
It was your clover-choked

windmills that threw me.
Anyone would understand.
Abasement is where I keep
my receipts.

Guide to Low Standards

1.
Lean your ribs into a corner
and shake like an old dog
and sure enough, you'll draw
his pointing finger and a shout.

He'll ask you
will you call the police?
Will you? Will you?
Just like the last one?

You must be faster than his snatching hand.

2.
Here is the chandelier of fur,
and here is the floor for a foxtrot.
Here a strangling fig
descends the blackened walls.

Here is the rotted spot in the floor,
and there a flash of scarlet, a cardinal
stashed in each corner. There are the other
slack mouths, before, and the whispers

from behind brocades. Sweaty underskirts
and the rips in the ribbons hid with pins.
Here comes the rouged sisterhood
who will swear you in.

3.
This cracked tile will do.

On the Way Out

I woke
in the burning
house of him.

I chose,
as one does,
that which was
precious and close,

but had to shed the body
curled up in the smoke.
The structure could not be saved.

Notes on Logistics, Scene 10

Ask the boys in the sound booth
for a boom mic over

a screaming woman. Her age
does not matter. Nor her race.

Whether she is pretty
or not or loves her husband

or is already missing an arm.
Whether she will be penned

with the others, or her mother
bent over the plough.

Whether the flame
in the lieutenant's hands

or a button on his coat.
Whether the crops catch.

Whether the smell of the smoke
reminds her or her children of hunger.

Picture Show

When rocks fly through teeth,
the teeth do not shatter with the sound
a falling wineglass makes in the movies,
though that's how teeth shatter in my mind,
where a pebble emerges from a glove
on the arm of a wrought-iron patio chair
to hurtle toward a smiling girl and boy
(in the foreground, facing us, by the cake)
and passes first through the back
of the girl's head—silently, as though
her head were a hologram, or a clever
accretion of smokes—then shards her face
into a sound effect flying outward and toward,
in the case of some pieces, the viewer.

The Ascetic Explains the Mess

Tea gone cold blackens.
Too long on the sill: refuses
to steam, feeling no longer craved.
Yet craved but feared, as one fears
bitter questions (rancid nutmeats,
blood undercooked), or as
one cannot bear to own abandon.

Too quick the grip—
porcelain's shrill mist—
falling edges
fang themselves,
as certain small
fierce animals
can easily kill a larger.

Trial of the Oblique Triangle: Building Permit #78

No mail-order kit—from fig leaves and wire,
a hunchbacked assembly of seven-fold wings.
Yes, we knew the blue-toed skink
would bite its lover's digits off,
so in captivity we supervised,
and twice repaired the water pump
to flow our solid mile of trench.
But let the record show I never
swung that pickaxe without gloves:
the discipline of guilt demands precision.
Left over? Not one screw. At tea,
she stroked the neck feathers, impressed.
She served us tarts and handed us the pliers.
So much for tools. So much for cleverness.

The Facts We Prefer

As it may be generous
to donate firewood

to a heretic's burning,
so the ascetic thrashes

against the hands
that love him,

lest they settle
between his ribs

and take hold,
like sleeping hawks

whose relaxed claws
grip the perch more tightly, immobile

as the eyes and mouths
of the dead (exhausted

by surprise, as we all will be):
open, finally ready to receive.

We sew them shut
for decency's sake.

Windy Season

Shed of rusting shovel blades.
Egg-halves clutch dry leaves beside,
nestled in a grass of iron flakes.
The dove above broods over, still,
with her soft breast many sleeps.
When we speak, we say nothing
but never. Is she unaware
of all but what's left to warm?
Or, as the dream-heavy ovals
plummet past the flowering pecans,
does she share what flickers under
the unfledged eyelids? Her silence a gift
whose dark ribbons we crave.

Spite

What speaks behind me
won't be silenced
by hair. I pluck,
from sunk to the gum
to a heel-dangle,
the toothy things
of my spine
and one by one,
detached,
set them to burn
and will not swerve
for their whelping,
cross-eyed wretches.

In the Smithy

Don't mind my doubtful face,
a few choice blows will right it—
tongs but a quarter-turn from the forge.

Striker at the hardy hole,
the smith minds his horn.
Red end—sudden drop—

flattened, my lips at the upsetting plate,
that I approach a throat of steam,
plunge my tongue in the voice of the crow.

Hammers, list a bit—
I'm to become anvil, hit
in the service of shaping a third thing.

3

What did you think, that joy
was some slight thing?

—Mark Doty

Urchin to Follow

I'm sending you this urchin for a reason, Smoke.
          —"Echinoidea Freddy," Mike Chasar

Because it is hollow, and its five parts compose
a whole that greens, transposed to garden,
once exposed to swampy air. Because it claims
its wishbones, five matched ramparts
grown round tongues of water, now of air,

each calling still to fortify
the walls of shell, lest they collapse
into the larger green. The urchin
a communal singularity, a solipsistic whole
whose diversified nerves dream the whole story,

down to the ocean's bones. I ride out
each green interval as a sailing rajah's
overboard thief, occupy the hollow beat
between wave and wave, leaf and leaf,
sink in the greening of my earliest wishes,

and wait to be cured of my errors.
Each wish composed of many parts.

Interview with the Rescue Crew

On a scale of one to five? I'm a half-of-me hanging out
of a flying saucer with a grin kind of woman.
I'm fresh-sprung from the groin vault,
and ready to pertain. I'm a spider monkey
upside-down under the stairs, woman.
I'm swinging from the plumbing pipes,
a woman grown from a girl who danced in suspenders.
Girl who wondered where to put her hands.

Regrets? I wished I'd lived through disco, slept with
mirror-ball dust in my dress, but I'm a fortunate woman
who has never lived under the threat of the coat hanger,
only a girl who learned the hard way that an easy laugh
makes people think you're flirting. A lemur-eyed kind.
A nervous-hair-twirling accidental coquette sneaking
to the kitchen to build pyramids of cheese,
assembling gentle forest creatures from the toothpicks.
Convinced I'll see the dead
if I should once let down my guard.
Hence my preference for early rising, when I can sleep
for my fear of green chairs and the clacking
of the abacus that tallies my abandonments.
For I have not been where I should be.
I have hid, alone, and been cravenly happy.

Well, snag my lip in a double-bent hook
and call me a spiny-finned so-and-so!
How long has it been since the last masked ball?
Whatever happened, I wonder,
to that little chimney sweep who lectured us
about the printing press of hell?
I tell you, I took comfort in your Jesus eyes
as we hid behind Madame d'Exupéry and her skirts,
admiring her prodigious calves.
Even then, you were compassionate
while maintaining boundaries,
whereas I am an entirely permeable membrane,
rent like a grumpy Bacchus whenever I enter a room.

You tease! I'll not be bit by a goose,
if that's what you mean.
As for cooperatives, none for me, never,
whether for painting or produce,
though I attend a shadow-puppet show now and then.
But I could love the back of any man's neck,
creased with the dirt the persimmon rind gives,
for I am sentient as an accumulation of fruit bowls.

O, speak again, bright angel!
Let us flee from this wine-and-cheese event,
and make sweetness in the broom closet.
  —Posh, you know everything I've ever said
to a department head was a lie.

And if you asked me about teaching,
whatever I said then, I lied to you too.
Even if you thought we were friends.
Even if you were right.

For I am a dropping all my papers
in the aisle of the bus woman,
trying to tote all my bags in one trip.
Stronger than I look and can pick up the end
of that couch woman,writing and twirling
all this and everything else too
without the aid of oenophiles.
Must blink thirty times
before you take the picture woman,
stationed on both coasts at once
but cannot find her keys.
Woman with a table overlooking the library. Ha!
Now I shall see how it's done.
Heaven help me! Dark bus stop
without enough light to read woman!
Woman with black widows under her coffee table,
shaking her planetary bells.
Woman alert to goddess power,
yet alarmed by people with drums.
Woman who ducks under dark lintels
to light votives only in cities where she does not live.

Woman who has outlived her ability
to deliver a convincing power ballad.

Woman behind the reception desk
who's drawing talking faces on her hands.
Woman who can tell an epiphyte from a fire barrel.
Woman of cedar and seafoam.
Woman quick and coy with kelp,
bedecking her fins with tambourines.
She who runs with limpets.
Hey, little bivalve, save some filtered mollusk love for me!
Woman who brings up the back of the parade.

Basta Così

To hell with the language's *bella figura*,
each knuckle separately gloved,
no touching. Each rib a line in the sand.

Enough disjunction. Your sounds cloud the air:
utter *pulse*, and your lips rush my throat.
List with me on the mist-slippery cobbles together—

I care not whom we scandalize,
so let words, which are bodies, reveal bodies.
Let the tongue, that arbiter of sweetness,

clot and finally fail, but in the meantime
savor the erotic
in a syntax that cleaves to relation.

Let's have a real old-fashioned
love poem, for Chrissakes!
Let us not settle for copulative verbs.

Let's have moonrise over the Mediterranean
and six tiny fishing boats
lighting their lamps and your head in my lap

and my hands in your hair
and you asking me please
to keep humming that old song,

because I am so good at it
and so beautiful
and such a comfort to you.

Epithalamium

—for Teggin and Robert Summers

Swallows gather at the lakemouth's fog:
　　nearly the hour of speech.
　　　　Under the shoreline gazebo's beams,
fan blades tick the light chain, keeping time
　　until the bridesmaids' heels
　　　　commence their clicking to a string quartet.
Dearly beloved, we are gathered
　　by the creak of folding chairs, green voices
　　　　from the shadows on the lawn.
How will she arrive, the bride, her long, long train?
　　Aboard a craft of wooden wheels,
　　　　into the flower girl's beckoning blooms;
stems crushed in the carriage spokes
　　release their scents to the groom.
　　　　Love, hold, honor, cherish, until: I will—
from *willan*: *I apply my will* and *I wish, desire*—
　　spilled on the tongue of the lake,
　　　　tasted in that slower world.

Reading and Writing on the Bus: How I Quit Missing My Stop and Learned to Love Pastiche

I'm standing at the cutting board chopping sage
and it hits me what it means that she is letting me
be in charge of the dressing: I am going to die.[1]

"So it is, so it is," said the Mole, with great heartiness.[2]

Let us begin with the problem of sight.
And place ourselves, like lovers, in darkness.[3]

If x is the number of times I say, "I will not come to you,"
and y is every tadpole you place in my hand
as the last snow melts from the riverbank,
then what we graph is a math of resistance.

As we consider the form-making capacity of poiēsis
for the creation of intersubjectivity, Levinas reminds us
of another fear, a fear that the necessity
of such activity is never-ending.[4]

At least those frilly blouses catch the wind.[5]

Cottleston, Cottleston, Cottleston Pie,

A fly can't bird, but a bird can fly.
Ask me a riddle and I reply:
"*Cottleston, Cottleston, Cottleston Pie.*"[6]

Chickens seem the obvious solution.[7]

To cleave: both to cling to
and to be parted from,
as by a sword or by water.

The way, rounding a corner
into a billow of lilac, that sweet
swarm to the back of the brain can wound.

On the platypus,
considering the invention of wine—

Both science and poetry proceed, in part,
by making pictures of what we cannot see . . .
by attributing corporeal qualities
to inscrutable events.[8]

Let's eat trailmix in our sleeping bags
and watch the deer piss in the river.

Our wildest dive strangely will unbind us,
though we have bound ourselves
as fence-wound winter vines,
we loosen always limb by limb

ourselves as music loosens
(sounding deeply, muscularly) its last mouth;
or if our desire be to bind ourselves,
we and our hopes will curl very beautifully, softly,
as when the bark of this grapevine rasps
against the wood's grain carefully curve-wise warping;
everything that we are to long for in this world pertains
to the undertow of our interdicted billow —

"Such a rumpus everywhere!" continued the Otter.[9]

You can barely find an olive tree to hang yourself from.[10]

Despite such admonitions, some people insist
on using snap shackles or other hardware
because it seems simpler.[11]

Hey! It's fall. It's time for rollerskates.
Some people go for style and grace.
Me, I like a quick Hail Mary
and a straight shot down a long hill.
It's better if you scream.

She paces the lawn as surfaces soften, concede,
as the fig's large-handed leaves shadow
the patio's stones. Long strokes of the bow,
slow notes: the same sad Gypsy tune on a loop.
Each note a honeyed needle, sweet, sweet.

As for measure and other technical apparatus,
that's just common sense:
if you're going to buy a pair of pants
you want them to be tight enough
so everyone will want to go to bed with you.[12]

Love doesn't require forgiveness. It favors tact
over honesty —

           A fistful of leaves, over none at all.[13]

Thus, as materialism has been generally taught,
it is utterly unintelligible.[14]

I was in charge of eighteen teenagers,
responsible not only for their lives,
but also for transforming them into a troupe
of gospel-spreading street mimes.[15]

Ice on the mast and in the beards
of the men holding hatchets.

Can the need to be torn apart be soberly said?[16]

The wind is rough tonight,
It blows the ocean's white hair.
I do not fear the fierce Vikings
Crossing the Irish Sea.[17]

Man is the only animal

of which I am thoroughly and cravenly afraid.[18]

They'd confused pleasure with the making of pleasure,
the way others mistake exactness of composition for
perfection, and call it art.[19]

Oh, dear! I don't know what it is. Love for the absent
don't sound like it; but try it, and see how it goes.[20]

The cowboys at college are roping
their metal steer in the parking lot again.

Desire as useless as the ten commandments
posted on a lawn: print too small to read from a car
on a street where nobody walks.

These are not the boas of my youth.

If cedars grew above me while I slept,
I'd know home by the smell of the dirt.

Her hand billows away from his shoulder
like a magnet meeting its mate
as the last birds break free of the juniper,
turn like a slapped profile—

Oh Lord, don't let my final rest
be across from The Barbecue Shack.

This was too much for Pippin.
His thoughts went back to the Field of Cormallen,
and here was a squint-eyed rascal
calling the Ring-bearer "little cock-a-whoop."[21]

There is an air of misanthropy
about the striped snake
that will commend itself at once to your taste, —[22]

No thank you, not even
to the Biscuit Barn.
No, not even for Jesus.

Nights curled in the rowboat bottom,
turning under a bat-filled sky.

Irreparable as a ripped wedding dress,
as impossible to part from.

In ourselves we house such noise and streamers.

Sorry —
Bell's broke —
Please hollar![23]

"I shan't call it the end,
till we've cleaned up the mess," said Sam gloomily.
"And that'll take a lot of time and work."[24]

NOTES

1. Sarah Vowell, "The First Thanksgiving," *The Partly Cloudy Patriot*

2. Kenneth Grahame, *The Wind in the Willows*

3. Frederick Leboyer, *Birth Without Violence*

4. Susan Stewart, *Poetry and the Fate of the Senses*

5. Danielle Pafunda, e-mail 10/29/07

6. A. A. Milne, *Winnie-the-Pooh*

7. Courtney Denney, in conversation 11/13/07

8. Daniel Tiffany, *Toy Medium: Materialism and Modern Lyric*

9. Kenneth Grahame, *The Wind in the Willows*

10. Heard on National Public Radio during a broadcast regarding European farm subsidies, 11/12/07

11. Daniel Spurr, *Your First Sailboat: How to Find and Sail the Right Boat for You*

12. Frank O'Hara, "Personism: A Manifesto"

13. Carl Phillips, "Stardust," *Riding Westward*

14. Samuel Taylor Coleridge, *Biographia Literaria*

15. Josh Andersen of Wayne, Pennsylvania, in a letter to the editors of *The Sun*, 11/07

16. Coleman Barks, "Walk Soup," *Winter Sky: New and Selected Poems, 1968–2008*

17. Written in the margin of a ninth-century Irish manuscript and printed as the epigraph in Patricia Aakhus's *The Voyage of Mael Duin's Curragh*

18. George Bernard Shaw, "In the Days of My Youth"

19. Carl Phillips, "Shall Want for Nothing," *Riding Westward*

20. Emily Dickinson, letter to Mrs. A. P. Strong, 1850

21. J. R. R. Tolkien, *The Return of the King*

22. Emily Dickinson, letter to Mrs. A. P. Strong, 1850

23. Sign at Sunshine Cleaners, Athens, GA, 10/09/07

24. J. R. R. Tolkien, *The Return of the King*

Evening

Winter wheat sleeps in sheaves.
The fur on all the animals is licked
in the same direction. Thin
in their gowns of ice, the lindens.
A plank for every adze.
Steam gathers shadows on the sill
and each grape sees itself in a glass.
Preserves.

We Lie Down at Last

The best eyes come from Germany;
someone curses gently in that tongue
as he breathes fire into focus,
a glass facsimile of sight

for those devoted taxidermists
who value the distinction
between antelope and oryx,
who strive to preserve

a still version
of each creature's variation on the vertical,
every aspiration to God's altitude,
by angling the eyes just so.

Where does the antelope stare
when the hunter brings it down?
The hunter who longs
to become what's solid in the liquid grass,

who kneels beside it
to measure fur's fading pleasure
with a flat palm. The pleasure
travels somewhere

when the gaze blinks out,
as all joy journeys in dream.
Dusk, leaning over
the draw of your breath

as the day's flutes lull to sleep,
like the men who kneel in the meadow,
I am waiting for some warning
of the knowledge stillness brings,

to feel the instant
between the shiver
of flesh under the hand
and the hush that follows,

to follow the long arc of the hush itself,
its blind, certain trajectory.

Notes from a Migration

This isn't the sort of present you open on the train.

Form A must be filed in triplicate.

Driving alone out of Augusta at night,
it's okay to listen to country.

Form B must be filed in blue igpay atinlay.

It's so good to be blond —
no one sees you coming.

People do know better.

If you don't like hot pink ostrich,
stick to the men's.

The olive nets are orange and turquoise.

I wouldn't dangle from that madrona,
if I were you.

Now he makes a tail look extraneous.

You have no idea

how many people you've never met
want you to marry me.

Vorrei due biglietti per Firenze, per favore.

Form C on the night of the year's ninth new moon.

Ay, Querido.

A "cat's head biscuit" is the size of
a cat's head.

Quoi?

Always send a thank you note.
Remember to include some coastlines
and some knots.

He pulled that branch into the picture.

Moi?

You can sit over there,
with all the other funny sluts.

There is no shorting out
the worry circuit.

How does she handle?

About like a sugar-coated brick.

Don't leave me behind
like an old Eskimo without teeth.

Je n'ai pas reussí á l'éxamen de la français.

The monkeys will pay to look at porn.

Do not refuse the Baptists too unkindly:
I hear they return with muffins.

Þæt wæs gōd cyning!

Be nice to the ladies in the cafeteria.

Tutti ragazzi!

The ski instructor's observations:
"You must have remarkable balance.
I've never seen anyone so out of control
stay up for so long."

Southern girls and their daddies: ick.

May I suggest an alligator pit?

The secret to pie crust
is the smallest amount of liquid
dispersed with the fewest strokes.

By the time spiders are big enough to eat birds—
Ои, траге́дия!

It is better to love him
less as a man, more as a human.

An insight is two bells and a handle in between.

A conjunction is a rhetorical device.

Given the contradictions of the J-stroke,
is it possible to make any forward progress
paddling a canoe alone?

A croissant and orange juice
over the Alps
can make up for almost anything.

Reader, I married him.

NOTES

The section 1 epigraph is from Stanley Kunitz's poem "Touch
Me," in *Passing Through: The Later Poems, New and Selected* (W.
W. Norton, 1995).

I like to think that "Ode to Doubt" reveals my longstanding
love of Neruda's odes.

In "Possible Song," the line "Song of sugar that ends in sand"
is derived from poet Chris Forhan's description of an undesir-
able wine, delivered at a dinner gathering in Athens, Georgia.
Forhan's poem "Sugar and Sand" appears in *Crazyhorse* #68,
and in his book *Black Leapt In* (Barrow Street Press, 2009).

The section 2 epigraph is from Donna Stonecipher's poem "The
Guest," in *The Reservoir* (University of Georgia Press, 2002).

The section 3 epigraph is from Mark Doty's poem "Visitation,"
in *Sweet Machine* (Harper Perennial, 1998).

"Interview with the Rescue Crew" was energized by Anne
Waldman's *Fast Speaking Woman* (City Lights Books, 1996).

In *"Basta Così,"* the phrase "arbiter of sweetness" is lifted from
a conversation with Deborah Miller, Associate Director of
First-Year Composition at the University of Georgia, who used
it to describe Administrative Coordinator Jane Barroso as "my
arbiter of sweetness."

In "Notes from a Migration," "Don't leave me behind / like an old Eskimo without teeth" is but one of many quotable class-room requests from Judith Ortiz Cofer, Regents' and Franklin Professor of English and Creative Writing at the University of Georgia.

In "Notes from a Migration," "Ои, трагéдия!" ("Oh, trag-edy!") was the preferred exclamation of Vladimir Gross, Senior Lecturer in the Department of Slavic Languages and Literature, upon hearing the recitations of his students, when I took his beginning Russian class at the University of Washington in 1993–4.

In "Notes from a Migration," "Þæt wæs gōd cyning!" is a bit of *Beowulf* (line 11), meaning "That was a good king!"

ACKNOWLEDGMENTS

I am grateful to the editors of the following publications, where these poems or earlier versions of them first appeared: *Coconut* ("You," "Ode to the Tune of Frank O'Hara," "The Facts We Prefer," "Basta Cosi"); *Convergence* ("Stance," "Road Trip"); *Court Green* ("Possible Song"); *Isotope* ("Marriage Song in the Desert"); *The Journal* ("Interview with the Rescue Crew"); *Los Angeles Review* ("Guide to Low Standards"); *Memorious* ("Ode to Doubt," "The Smithy"); *Naugatuck River Review* ("Road Trip"); *New Delta Review* ("Notes from a Migration"); *Ninth Letter* ("What the Evening Requires"); *Protest Poems* ("Notes on Logistics, Scene 10"); *Red Clay Review* ("Advice," "We Lie Down at Last"); *Redheaded Stepchild* ("To the Rescue Crew"); *Sacramento News & Review* ("Urchin to Follow," "Trial of the Oblique Triangle: Building Permit #78"); *Santa Clara Review* ("Stance"); *Sin Fronteras* ("Homecoming Weekend"); *Sakura Review* ("Tracking the Woodcutter"); *Sojourn* 21 (2008) ("Gringos Lost in the Sonoran Desert"); and *Terrain.org: A Journal of the Built & Natural Environments* ("Epithalamium").
*

"Ode to Doubt" appears in *Breathe: 101 Contemporary Odes* (C&R Press, 2009).
*

"Possible Song" won a Dorothy Sargent Rosenberg Memorial Poetry Prize in 2005; "Possible Song," "Advice," and "The Facts We Prefer" together received an honorable mention from the *Atlantic Monthly* Student Writing Contest in 2005; "Notes from a Migration" won the Matt Clark Poetry Prize from the *New Delta Review* in 2007.

*

Many of these poems were completed with the support of a fellowship from the University of Georgia.

*

Many thanks to my family, word people one and all. I am indebted to generous teachers, among them Heather McHugh, Chris Forhan, Connie Voisine, and Judith Ortiz Cofer. I have leaned on my friends and mentors, especially Rachel Whalley, Liz Green, Tim Staley, Valerie Fioravanti, Siân Griffiths, Jenn Blair, Misha Cahnmann Taylor, David Ingle, Mindy Wilson, and Regan Huff, for poetry sympathy and strategy, and I have stolen the best phrases of my friends' and colleagues' conversation. C. J. Sage exemplifies editorial energy, insight, and tact. I thank my darling husband, Dorje, for his support and atmosphere of ease.